Improving
SPEED

Paul Mason

WAYLAND

First published in 2010 by Wayland

Copyright © Wayland 2010

Wayland
Hachette Children's Books
338 Euston Road
London NW1 3BH

Wayland Australia
Level 17/207 Kent Street
Sydney, NSW 2000

Editor: Julia Adams
Designer: Tim Mayer, Mayer Media
Picture researcher: Kathy Lockley
Proofreader and indexer: Claire Shanahan
Consultant: Professor John Brewer

British Library Cataloguing in Publication Data

Mason, Paul, 1967-
   Training for sport.
   Improving speed.
   1. Running speed--Juvenile literature. 2. Physical
   fitness--Nutritional aspects--Juvenile literature.
   I. Title
   613.7'1-dc22

ISBN 9780750261432

Printed in China

Wayland is a division of Hachette Children's Books,
an Hachette UK company.

www.hachette.co.uk

Websites
The website addresses (URLs) included in this book were
valid at the time of going to press. However, because of the
nature of the Internet, it is possible that some addresses may
have changed, or sites may have changed or closed down
since publication. While the author and publisher regret any
inconvenience this may cause the readers, no responsibility
for any such changes can be accepted by either the author
or the publisher.

Disclaimer
During the preparation of this book, all due care has been
taken with regard to the advice, activities and techniques
described and depicted. The publishers regret that they can
accept no liability for any loss or injury sustained.

Picture acknowledgements:
David R. Anchuelo/Real Madrid via Getty Images: 20
Dmitry Argunov/Shutterstock: COVER (small, top)
Tengku Bahar/AFP/Getty Images: 11
Guillaume Baptiste/AFP/Getty Images: 27
Bon Appetit/Alamy: 28
Shaun Botterill/Getty Images: 7
Clive Brunskill/Getty Images: 26
Martin Bureau/AFP/Getty Images: 13
Kenneth William Caleno/Shutterstock: 18
Schmid Christophe /Shutterstock: COVER (small, middle)
Bob Elsdale/Photonica/Getty Images: Title page, 8
Stu Forster/Getty Images: 17
Eric Gaillard/Reuters/Corbis: 29
Jesse D. Garrabrant/NBAE via Getty Images: 21
John Gichigi/Getty Images: Cover (main), 24
VOJTa Herout/Shutterstock: background throughout
AdrianHillman/iStock images: folios throughout
Heinz Kluetmeier/Sports Illustrated/Getty Images: 6
Byn Lennon/Getty Images: 9
Alex Livesey/Getty Images: 14
Chris McGrath/Getty Images: 10
Hughes Martin/Corbis: 19
Pedro Jorge Henriques Monteiro/Shutterstock:
          COVER (small, bottom)
Olivier Morin/AFP/Getty Images: 5
Pascal Pavani/AFP/Getty Images: 15
Clive Rose/Getty Images: 16
Pixel Sculler/Alamy: 4
Franck Seguin/TempSport/Corbis: 25
Serghei Starus/Shutterstock: background throughout
Kirk Treakle/Alamy: 22
Suzanne Tucker/Shutterstock: background throughout
Phil Water/Getty Images: 23

Contents

The need for speed

Some people are naturally speedy. These people's bodies come equipped with lots of the elements that allow humans to do things quickly. But don't despair if you're not one of them. With some insider knowledge, anyone can train themselves to be faster!

Basics of speed

This book is about what makes sportspeople speedy. Speed is made up of several elements. These include:

- **Strength:** the amount of force you are able to put into moving. Speed events require this force, which comes from the muscles, to be generated quickly.

Some people start off naturally speedier than others. But even the runner at the back would get faster with some specialist speed training!

- **Technique:** how efficiently the force gets turned into movement. An important part of this is flexibility – your joints being able to make all the movements that are needed.

Events based on pure speed don't usually take much time: the athletes go fast, but they don't do it for very long. Top 100-metre sprinters, for example, spend less than 10 seconds on the track. It's not an easy option, though: they still have to train for hours each day!

Sports such as football, basketball or rugby have an added element. The players have to be speedy, in order to out-run opponents or get into good positions quickly. But they have to do it again and again during the course of a game. This kind of speed requires a third building block:

- **Speed endurance:** how well you are able to stay at, or keep coming back to, near-maximum speed over a set period of time.

'The Lightning Bolt', Usain Bolt crosses the line way ahead of his rivals at the 2008 Olympic Games. At 1.98 m tall, Bolt is unusually big for a sprinter.

Usain Bolt

Sport: 100 m and 200 m sprinting

Country: Jamaica

Born: 21 August 1986

Usain Bolt is the miracle man of modern athletics. He is the fastest sprinter in the world over 100m and 200m, and has set multiple word records in both events.

Bolt first became a superstar at the 2008 Beijing Olympics. Despite slowing down towards the end of the race, and having a shoelace undone, he set a new 100 m world record of 9.69 seconds. Then he also broke the record for 200 m, which had stood for an amazing 12 years.

A year later, Bolt was back. At the World Championships in Berlin, he shaved over a tenth of a second off the old 100 m record – leaving some commentators speechless in disbelief. In the 200 m, Bolt ran 19. 19 seconds, and won by the biggest distance in World Championship history.

Types of speed

What do we mean when we talk about speed? Most people immediately think of going as fast as possible. This is called top speed, or sprint speed. It is important in full-speed events such as the 100 m on track, 50 m in the pool, and 1000 m in the velodrome. Top speed is one kind of speed – but not the only one.

Acceleration speed

In sports such as football, rugby, basketball, hockey and water polo, the players have to be able to accelerate through defences, keep up with attackers, block off space, and so on. In some sports, this acceleration to top speed is more important than the top speed itself. One example comes from basketball. Through proper training, a player might be capable of reaching 30 km/h on a 60 m-long track. But it would do them no good on a basketball court, which is only 28.65 m long.

The player will do better by training to reach a speed of, say, 25 km/h in 10 metres. This kind of acceleration speed is important in many team sports, where players are often competing with an opponent to reach a space on the pitch or gain territory before their opposite number.

Reaction speed

Imagine someone throwing a punch at your head. You don't think to yourself, "Uh oh! Now I should duck." You just duck. That kind of fast, unthinking movement is called reaction speed. Fast reactions are important in sports such as boxing, kart racing, judo and downhill mountain biking.

Body-part speed

Some sports require speed from a particular body part. Think of athletes throwing the javelin, or tennis players serving. They need rapid movement from one body part, their arm. They train for this single movement, but they also train their whole body for speed. This is because their throwing or serving movement relies on other muscles all over the body.

The explosive power of sprinters at the start of a 100 m race. This is the women's semi-final at the 2008 Beijing Olympics.

Fastest players in the Premiership

In 2008, a sportswear company put together figures showing which players in the English Premier League were quickest. There are two numbers for each player: first their speed getting to the ball, then running with it:

1 Cristiano Ronaldo: 20.9/20.8 m/h
2 Andrew Johnson: 20.6/20.7
3 Fernando Torres: 20.5/20.6
4 Kenwyne Jones: 20.7/20.2
5 Ashley Young: 20.4/20.3
6 Aaron Lennon: 20.6/19.6
7 Cameron Jerome: 20.3/20.1
8 Shaun Wright-Phillips: 18.9/21.2
9 Jermain Defoe: 20.4/19.2
10 David Bentley: 20.0/19.8

Theo Walcott

Sport: Football

Country: England

Born: 21 August 1986

Theo Walcott has been a household name since he was selected as part of England's World Cup squad in 2006 – at just 17 years old. Walcott did not play in any matches, but has gone on to be one of the brightest stars in the Premier League and the England team.

Walcott has always been spoken of as one of the fastest footballers around. In 2009, he was clocked at 35 km/h in a speed test. It compares well with Usain Bolt's 24.04 m/h in the final of the 100 m at the 2009 World Championships.

The result made Walcott the Premiership's fastest-ever footballer. He would be capable of running a world-class 9.9 seconds for the 100 m if he was able to keep it up, but Walcott's training is for bursts of acceleration, not sustained top speed.

Theo Walcott shows a turn of speed, and escapes from a defender during an England match.

Muscles for speed

Speed requires power. In a fast car or motorbike, the power comes from the engine. In humans, the power comes from our muscles. All muscles are not the same, though: some are better at generating speed than others.

How muscles work

The muscles that move our limbs, allowing us to run, jump and throw things, work by contracting. They bunch up, pulling the two ends of the muscle together. This moves a joint, such as the knee or elbow. Every movement we make relies on muscles in this way.

In judo, sensing when your opponent is off balance is one thing. You also need fast muscle reactions to seize the opportunity for a throw.

Bigger muscles are able to move the joint with more force than smaller ones, and provide more power. It's a bit like having a car with a bigger engine than everyone else's – you can go faster than them!

Muscle speed

Power alone isn't enough for speed-based athletes. They also need to get the power out quickly. To see why, imagine the rhythm of a 60 m sprinter's feet: *rat-tat-tat-tat-tat-tat*! If the rhythm of the runner's footfalls was *per-dunk… per-dunk… per-dunk…* they wouldn't run as quickly, however much power went into each step. How quickly your muscles can put out power depends on what type of fibre they are made of.

Muscle fibres

There are two main types of skeletal muscle:
1) slow-twitch muscles, which provide power slowly but for a long time, and are ideal for endurance sports.

2) fast-twitch muscles, which provide power quickly (contracting 5–10 times quicker than slow-twitch muscles), but not for very long. Fast-twitch muscles are ideal for speed-based sports.

We are all born with different proportions of slow- and fast-twitch fibres in our muscles. Most people are in the range 45–55 per cent fast-twitch and 45–55 per cent slow-twitch. Those with more fast-twitch fibres are likely to be naturally speedier.

Mark Cavendish wins one of his record haul of six stage victories in the 2009 Tour de France.

Mark Cavendish

Sport: Cycling

Country: UK

Born: 21 May 1985

Mark Cavendish is one of the biggest stars in cycling. He styles himself as the fastest sprinter in the profession: "If I'm in front with 200 metres to go, there's nobody who can beat me", he says. Few of his rivals disagree.

Sprint finishes in bicycle stage races place incredible demands on the rider's body:
- With about 5 km to go, Cavendish's team moves to the front of the race. They keep the pace high – up to 60 km/h – so that no one can break away.
- Cavendish's teammates take turns at the front of the line of riders, each peeling away as he is exhausted. Cavendish shelters at the back.
- 550 m from the finish, only Cavendish and his lead-out man, Mark Renshaw, are left. Renshaw sprints at full speed to 180 m from the line.
- As Renshaw peels off, Cavendish launches himself towards the line at speeds nudging 80 km/h.

Cavendish first hit the headlines during the 2008 *Tour de France*, when he won four sprint finishes. Then, in the 2009 *Tour*, he went even better, winning a record six stages. Already, at just 24, Cavendish had become a cycling legend.

Building up power

Muscle power is crucial for sprinting, whether it's on foot, a bike, or in the pool. Power is a combination of the force your muscles can exert (their strength) and the speed with which they can contract.

Types of strength

In sports, there are three different kinds of strength, which combine in slightly different ways, depending on the sport you play:

1) Maximum strength: the greatest force that is possible in a single muscle contraction. Maximum strength is most important in power sports, such as weightlifting or Strongman contests.

2) Elastic strength: the ability to overcome resistance with a fast muscle contraction. Elastic strength is important at the start of a sprint, and in combat sports such as judo or wrestling.

3) Strength endurance: the ability to express force many times over. Strength endurance is important in sports such as basketball, football or swimming, where you have to make the same movements again and again.

Strength training

Strength training makes muscles able to generate more force. It does this by overloading the muscles, working them harder than they normally would. Most top sportspeople do this through weight training, which forces the muscles to contract against greater resistance than normal. There are two key benefits of strength training:

Top athletes from almost all sports use weight training as a way of increasing their strength and power.

1) increases the size of the fibres that make up your muscles. This is known as muscle hypertrophy. The muscle also develops a slightly different chemical structure, and becomes better able to retain glycogen.

2) repeats the same muscle movement again and again. This makes the central nervous system better at responding, so the movement becomes more efficient and effective.

They increase the power available from the muscles, particularly fast-twitch muscles. Popular plyometric exercises include:

- straight-leg jump, using your ankles and calves to spring into the air

- spring jogging, leaping as high and far as possible with each stride

- depth jumps, stepping off a box or bench 40–80 cm high, then leaping straight up into the air (jumping from a greater height increases strength, lower height increases speed)

- plyometric press-ups, where you push up fast enough for your hands to leave contact with the floor, then immediately do the next press-up when you land

Power training and plyometrics

Strength alone is no use in speed-based sports: it has to be combined with fast muscle movement. These two together are known as power. One way to develop power is through exercises called plyometrics.

Plyometric exercises involve rapid contraction and relaxation of the muscles, in the same way as many sports.

Plyometric exercises put significant strain on the body, so must only be done when supervised by a qualified coach or PE teacher.

Energy for speed

If your muscles are like a car's engine, powering it along, what does the engine run on? The human engine runs on a substance called ATP. When the muscles ask for energy, the body breaks down ATP into a second substance, called ADP. It is this breaking-down process that provides energy.

Energy stores

The body stores energy in two key forms: carbohydrates and fats. Carbohydrates are stored in your muscles and liver, and fats are stored under your skin, and around your major organs.

Both carbohydrates and fats can be used to produce ATP, but fats are a slow-burning energy source that is not useful in speed-based events. For speed, the key energy source is a type of carbohydrate called glycogen.

Energy production

The body produces energy to power its muscles in two key ways:

1) Anaerobic energy production happens without the need for oxygen. Anaerobic activity produces energy very quickly, but also uses a lot of muscle glycogen. Athletes operating at or near their maximum speed or acceleration are always using the anaerobic energy system.

There are two different anaerobic energy systems. The first provides up to six seconds

Excercise intensity and energy source

The energy source your body uses depends on what percentage of your maximum heart rate (MHR; the most number of times your heart can beat in one minute) you are exercising at:

Intensity % MHR	% Carbohydrate	% Fat
65 to 70	40	60
70 to 75	50	50
75 to 80	65	35
80 to 85	80	20
85 to 90	90	10
90 to 95	95	5
100	100	0

Aerobic vs. anaerobic energy sports

This table shows what percentage of aerobic and anaerobic energy athletes in different sports and events use:

Activity:	Aerobic energy:	Anaerobic energy:
Marathon	98%	2%
Track 1500 m	50%	50%
Field hockey	20%	80%
Track sprint 200 m	5%	95%
Baseball	0%	100%
Basketball	0%	100%
Football: goalkeeper	0%	100%
Football: forward	0%	100%

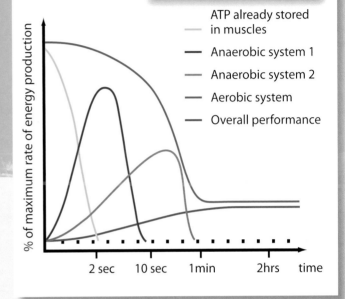

This graph shows how different energy systems kick in and then fall away during a single minute of flat-out exercise.

of energy, and is crucial in sports where an explosion of power is needed, such as weightlifting. The second provides energy for up to 90 seconds, and is important for other speed-based sports.

2) Aerobic energy production happens in the presence of oxygen. This produces energy relatively slowly, but also uses glycogen very efficiently. Aerobic energy production is most important in endurance sports, when the athletes have to keep going for a long time.

Limited energy stores

The body is only able to store a limited amount of energy. Most coaches say that athletes exercising aerobically will run out of muscle glycogen after approximately two hours. Athletes exercising anaerobically use up their muscle glycogen more quickly (in about 90 seconds), because anaerobic exercise uses glycogen far more rapidly.

At the end of a big race, even the great swimmer Michael Phelps has exhausted his anaerobic energy resources and run out of power. The resulting discomfort is clear to see.

Speed endurance

Speed endurance is the ability to keep using your power over a period of time. The longer a speed event goes on, the greater an athlete's speed endurance needs to be. So, for example, a 100 m sprinter relies less on speed endurance than a 400 m runner. Speed endurance has two key components: anaerobic endurance and aerobic endurance.

Anaerobic endurance

In any fast movement lasting up to about 90 seconds, most of the body's energy is produced anaerobically (without the need for oxygen). This uses up the energy stored in the muscles very quickly, which is why it is difficult to go at top speed for a long time. After a brief rest, though, the body's systems start to recharge, ready for the next sprint.

Sports people can train their bodies so that their muscles become better at recharging with energy. They do this by repeatedly training for a short distance at maximum or near-maximum effort. The increased recharge ability is useful for lots of different athletes. Just think of how many sprints rugby players, footballers or netball players have to make, for example.

Spanish tennis pro Rafael Nadal sprints across court after making a return shot.

Fartlek Training

These players from the 2006 French team are doing Fartlek training. The ups, downs and sudden changes of the woods force them to regularly change their pace.

The amusingly named Fartlek training was developed in the 1930s, by a Swedish coach called Gösta Holmér. It is an excellent way of building up a combination of aerobic and anaerobic fitness.

Fartlek training relies on continuous movement, but at varied speeds. It is generally associated with running, but can be adapted to almost any sport that needs a combination of speed and endurance. It is adapted by matching it to the type of activity that takes place during competition.

After warming up, the athlete runs/cycles/swims/rows at a variety of speeds. They never slow to a complete stop, but never reaches maximum effort. The variation in pace draws energy from the aerobic and anaerobic energy systems in varied proportions.

Lactic acid

One of the by-products of anaerobic energy production is lactic acid, which produces a burning feeling in the muscles. If too much lactic acid builds up, the muscles stop working properly. Training increases the body's ability to remove lactic acid from the muscles.

Aerobic endurance

As exercise goes on for longer, the body relies increasingly on aerobic (with oxygen) energy.

At 95 per cent of maximum effort:

- for the first 10 seconds, your body uses 94 per cent anaerobic energy

- for the first minute, it uses 55 per cent anaerobic energy

- in 2 minutes of exercise, only 37 per cent of the energy is anaerobic; 63% is aerobic.

This means that athletes in speed-based events need a decent level of aerobic fitness. Their heart and lungs need to be good at transporting oxygen-rich blood to the muscles, and transporting away waste products.

Principles of speed training

How can coaching improve your speed? The details vary from sport to sport, from running to cycling, swimming or rowing. But there are general principles that can be applied to improving speed, whatever the sport.

Setting goals

First, coaches set their athletes a goal for an event. The athlete's speed training will then be done at higher speeds than this, but over shorter distances.

Decreasing rests

At first, the coach sets a long rest after each run/ride/swim. It may be as long as the run itself, or even longer. As the athlete gets fitter and faster, the coach allows shorter rests. This makes training increasingly like racing.

In endurance races such as this cycling sprint, starting too fast is a bad idea. It could cause a build-up of lactic acid in the muscles.

At this point, the coach may also spend more time overall on speed training. It is important, though, that the quality of the training does not drop off. The athlete must still be able to make the target times.

Race pace

The coach will also add in some training at the speed that will be required during the race (called 'race pace'). This gets the athlete's body used to what it feels like to move at the right speed. It improves their coordination, technique and endurance at the necessary speed.

Endurance and flexibility

As well as pure speed work, coaches will include training for endurance and flexibility. Easier-paced training over longer distances builds endurance and helps your body to recover from speed training. Flexibility helps develop a better range of movement for your chosen sport and event. This will increase speed and make injuries less likely.

Danny Cipriani

Sport: Rugby

Country: UK

Born: 2 November 1987

Danny Cipriani is one of the biggest talents in rugby. He is popular among rugby fans for his attacking flair and unusual ability to accelerate past defenders and through gaps.

As a teenager, Cipriani could have chosen to play more than one sport as a professional. He played youth football for Queens Park Rangers, and was offered a contract by Reading FC. He also had the chance to play cricket for Surrey. But Cipriani chose rugby: he broke into the Wasps team at just 17, and was playing for England by the time he was 21.

Cipriani has always made speed an important part of his game. He has trained for years with the sprint coach Margot Wells. Today, Wells coaches a long list of track athletes, rugby and hockey players, as well as running course for coaches. She describes the idea that great sprinters are born as a myth, and says that anyone can be trained to run fast.

Danny Cipriani of Wasps uses his speed to escape the clutches of a would-be tackler, who is left scrabbling at his ankles.

Building a training programme

You want to improve your performance, but how do you go about achieving your aims? Whatever event or sport you take part in, you need to plan out a training programme. This should to be based on two key things: what you have done before, and what is necessary for you to reach your goal.

Realistic goals

The most crucial part of a training programme is to set realistic goals. You might hope to swim 100 m freestyle in 56 seconds next year – but if your best time to date is 59 seconds, that's probably unrealistic. A better aim might be 57.5 seconds. You can then base your training plan around swimming that time one year from now.

Goals you can achieve

A big goal, such as improving your 100 m time, can be intimidating. To make it less so, it is important to set yourself smaller, less scary goals along the way. Top athletes break training programmes down into three 'cycles', or periods of time. This is a way of organising training into achievable goals:

- Long cycles: your long cycle should have big goals – for example, knocking 1.5 seconds off your 100 m time. These cycles last a long time. This could be the 11 months until the next schools championship.

- Medium cycles: break the long cycle up into several medium cycles. These shorter periods of time are spent doing something that will help you reach the big goal.

The first medium cycle, for example, might aim to build your strength or endurance.

- Short cycles: break the medium cycle into even shorter periods of time (usually weeks). During these periods, athletes do training that will help them reach their medium-cycle goal.

Training in a group has lots of benefits: it makes it easier to motivate yourself, and you get pulled (or pushed) along by faster athletes.

Training time and facilities

Be realistic about the amount of time you can spend training and what you can achieve. Full-time athletes can spend a vast amount of time training, so they make bigger improvements than those who can only spare an hour a day.

You also need to be realistic about the facilities that are available. For example, designing a training programme that includes three gym sessions a week is no use if you live 20 km from the nearest gym. Instead, your programme will need to include other kinds of strength work.

In sport, there are no shortcuts. If you want to get better at something, you have to train for it. Sometimes, it can be a long process.

A year in training

This general outline is a good starting place for developing a yearly training plan. It can be adapted to most sports, in particular track and field athletics, swimming and cycling.

• **First 16 weeks**
Each week should be spent improving your strength, flexibility, endurance and basic technique.

• **Second eight weeks**
Now the training programme moves to develop specific fitness (for example, explosive power for a 100 m sprinter, speed endurance for a 200 m swimmer). You should also work on finessing your technique.

• **Third eight weeks**
This is where things start to get interesting! You need a combination of training and competition experience. Training is partly to aid recovery from the efforts of competition, and partly to improve performance and technique.

• **Fourth eight weeks**
Train to maintain fitness, and polish technique as a result of what you have learned in the previous eight weeks.

• **Fifth eight weeks**
This period leads up to the main competition of the year. Include a combination of training and competition similar to the third eight weeks, but with adjustments made as a result of experiences earlier in the year.

• **Final four weeks**
Just do light training and recovery – and start planning next year's goals!

Warming up and cooling down

Whatever kind of training you are about to do, if you don't have time to warm up – don't train! However keen you are to get straight into the hard training, warming up first helps prevent injuries, and makes sure the body gets maximum benefit from training.

Continuous training

A good warm-up takes 15–30 minutes. Coaches tailor warm-ups to their athletes' needs, but most warm-ups for strength and power training should contain these three phases:

- **Phase 1**

  The warm-up starts with 5–10 minutes of exercise at a pace that increases the heart and breathing rate. The right pace is one at which you just begin to sweat.

- **Phase 2**

  Next, athletes mobilise their major joints and stretch key muscle groups, by repeatedly taking them through their entire range of movement. Examples include arm circles and knee bends.

- **Phase 3**

  Finally, athletes spend 5–10 minutes working on technique. They may gradually increase the load they put themselves under during this part of the warm-up.

Benefits of warming up

The increased blood flow and raised muscle temperatures caused by warming up have several benefits:

- **Preparing the body**
  Whilst resting, muscles only get about

These football players are warming up on a static bike, before they take part in a gym-based training session.

15 per cent of total blood flow. During exercise, they may demand up to 80 per cent. Warming up prepares the body for these demands.

- **Increased speed of movement**
  Warmed-up muscles are able to contract and relax more quickly. They have less resistance to movement. Signals to muscles from the nervous system are faster at higher temperatures, and the joints are able to move more freely.

• **Preventing injury**

Muscles that have not been warmed up before being asked to do hard work are less elastic. This makes them more likely to be damaged during exercise.

Cooling down

Most athletes cool down using 5–10 minutes of gentle exercise, followed by a further 5–10 minutes of stretching. Cooling down helps your body to recover from training or competition more quickly. It gives your body a chance to start getting rid of waste products released during training, and reduces the chances of your muscles later becoming sore.

Derrick Rose accelerates into the scoring zone, in a 2009 match against the Boston Celtics.

Derrick Rose

Sport: Basketball

Country: USA

Born: 4 October 1988

Derrick Rose is a point guard for the Chicago Bulls NBA basketball team. He is also arguably the fastest basketball player in the world.

Rose's quality was clear from his first season in the NBA in 2008–09. He became the first Bulls player since the legendary Michael Jordan to score 10 points or more in his first 10 matches. Rose rounded off the season by winning the Rookie of the Year contest, as well as the annual NBA Skills Challenge.

Most top basketball players are giants, and at 1.92 m, Rose is on the small side. But what he lacks in size, he makes up for in speed. Rose is famed for his ability to cover ground faster than any other player. Defenders find it hard to keep up with his darting runs and inside covers.

Technique

Try cycling up a hill as far forward on the saddle as possible. Keep your arms bent, and look down at the front wheel. Then do the same ride sitting as far back on the saddle as possible, with almost straight arms and looking ahead. You'll do the ride faster – because you have used better technique. Technique – how you perform a physical movement – is crucial to speed.

Good technique equals speed

What makes one way of doing something 'good technique' for going fast, but another way 'bad technique'?

Good technique uses the most powerful muscles possible. Try kicking a ball moving only your foot – it doesn't go far. You are only using only the relatively small muscles around your ankle. Kick a ball using your whole leg, and it goes much further, because you are using the big muscles in your calf and thigh.

In addition, good technique uses the minimum amount of energy possible. A good snowboarder can gain speed on a slope using very little energy. Meanwhile, a bad one will go slower *and* use more energy.

Developing technique

Few people are born with perfect technique. Fortunately, though, any technique can be learned and improved. There are two key building blocks to developing your technique in any sport:

1) mental preparation: it is important to understand what you are trying to do and how it should feel

2) physical preparation: training to make the exact physical movement that is needed.

Many athletes find it helpful to use visualisation. They watch other people with ideal technique, then imagine themselves using those exact same movements.

In kendo classes like this one, the students repeat the same movements over and over again, as a way of improving their reaction times.

Start slow, finish fast

Technique cannot be learned using high-speed movements. At first, new movements are learned slowly. They may even be broken down into different parts. Even the simplest judo throw, for example, can be broken down into the grip, and the movements of the arms, head, upper body, hips, legs and feet. Once each of these elements can be done together perfectly at slow speed, the judoka begins to move faster and faster. The technique becomes automatic and the speed increases, until the technique is lightning-fast and can be used in competition.

Shanaze Reade leaps ahead in the semi-finals at the 2008 Beijing Olympics.

Fatigue

Tiredness, or fatigue, can have a big impact on technique. Fatigue makes the muscles start to behave differently because they are running out of energy. This is a vicious cycle: fatigue makes it increasingly difficult to keep good technique, so more energy is used for the same (or less) speed, which increases fatigue.

Shanaze Reade

Sport: Cycling

Country: UK

Born: 23 September 1988

Shanaze Reade is one of the hottest properties in cycling. The winner of two elite world BMX titles and two world track cycling titles by the time she was 20, Reade is destined to be at the top of her sport for many years.

Reade began competing in BMX races at the age of 10. She was soon racing against, and beating, the boys. By 2006, she was the top British BMX rider in the 19-and-over men's category – despite being a woman, and only 17! In 2007 and 2008, she won world BMX titles.

In 2007, just a month after first competing in a velodrome, Reade and Victoria Pendleton won a gold medal at the World Track Championships. They then repeated the amazing win the following year.

Flexibility

However powerful your muscles are, you wouldn't be able to move very fast if you could only lift your knees up a few centimetres. Being able to move joints such as your knees, hips and elbows a long way is called being flexible. Good flexibility is crucial if you want to develop good technique.

What controls flexibility?

Flexibility is mainly determined by how good your muscles are at relaxing and lengthening. Imagine a boxer trying to side-step a punch. The muscles on the right side of their neck tighten up, pulling the head to the right. At the same time, the muscles on the left relax. If they relax quickly and into a long shape, the boxer's head moves further to the right, and they have a better chance of not being hit!

Big muscles that have been built up for strength and power sometimes develop a limited range of movement. Careful training can prevent this:

- It is important for speed-based athletes to use the same range of movement when overloading their muscles (for example during weight training) as they would use in competition.

- Stretching exercises can be used to increase the flexibility of muscles and joints.

Limits on flexibility

There are limits to how flexible each of us is. It's important to bear these limits in mind, or there is a risk of pushing joints beyond what is possible.

- Age has an effect: young people generally start off more flexible than older people

- Females are usually more flexible than males

- Warmer temperatures allow increased flexibility

- Most people are more flexible in the afternoon or evening than in the morning

Hurdlers are just one example of athletes who have to combine speed and flexibility if they are going to be successful.

Everyone can improve their flexibility, but not everyone is equally flexible. Never push harder than is comfortable because you are trying to copy someone else. Flexibility training may be mildly uncomfortable, but should never be painful.

Alexander Popov in training. Popov's long reach and incredible 'hold' on the water helped him set a world record for the 50 m freestyle.

Alexander Popov

Sport: Swimming

Country: Russia

Born: 16 November 1971

Alexander Popov is one of the greatest sprint swimmers of all time. His story is especially remarkable because he recovered from a near-fatal stabbing to return to the top of his sport.

At the Barcelona Olympics in 1992, Popov won gold in the 50 m and 100 m freestyle. Four years later, at the Atlanta Games, he repeated the victories. A month later, Popov was fighting for his life. He had been stabbed by a Moscow street stallholder. Only emergency surgery saved his life, and it took three months of treatment for him to recover.

Amazingly, in 1997 Popov won the European 50 m and 100 m titles. He won the same events at the 2003 World Championships, marking over a decade at the top of the most competitive events in swimming.

Popov is now a member of the International Olympic Committee, and is active in sports politics.

Reaction times

A starting signal goes off… or the back tyre on your kart starts to slide out… or your opponent tries to throw you over her shoulder and score *ippon*. How quickly you react could mean the difference between victory and defeat. That's why fast reactions are important in many different sports.

Developing your reactions

What are reactions? Put simply, your brain receives a signal that something has happened, such as a starting gun going off. It then sends a signal through your body's central nervous system to the muscles, saying that a physical action ("Start running!") is needed.

Some people naturally have fast reactions; others aren't so lucky. But the good news is that everyone can improve their reaction times:

- Practising the same reaction – for example, rehearsing the start of a race again and again – improves reaction speed.

- Specific sports also have their own drills to develop the fast reactions demanded in competition.

Influences on reaction speed

An athlete's reactions are influenced by a variety of conditions, some of which they may not be able to control:

- **The number of incoming signals**
  A racing driver responding to a start light will have faster reactions than a karate fighter who has to watch out for kicks and punches from both right and left.

Ready… steady… You need lightning reactions like the Williams sisters to return a serve that comes zinging towards you at 160 km/h.

- **Body temperature**
  A warmer body has faster reactions.

- **Sex and age**
  Young children have slow reactions, but these get quicker as they get older. Most people's reaction times peak at the age of about 17, then steadily get slower again. Males tend to have faster reactions than females.

- **Personality and mental state**
  Extroverts (people who enjoy being the centre of attention) tend to have quick reactions. People who are excited or concentrating very hard also have faster reactions.

Lewis Hamilton

Sport: Motor racing

Country: UK

Born: 7 January 1981

Lewis Hamilton is one of the hottest properties in motorsports. He was the youngest world champion in Formula One history, and is famous for his aggressive driving style and lightning-like reactions inside the cockpit of his race car.

Hamilton exploded onto the F1 circuit in 2007, with a debut season like nothing that had ever happened before. He won four races, and was beaten to the championship by a single point.

In 2008, Hamilton came back stronger, this time winning five races and winning the championship by a single point. In 2009, Hamilton was hampered by a car much slower than the competition, but still managed to win two races and come 5th in the drivers' championship.

Lewis Hamilton in the lead at the Italian Grand Prix in 2009.

Nutrition and hydration

What athletes eat and drink has a big effect on their training and performance in competition. Consuming the right food and drink helps them go faster. It fuels training efforts and makes sure they have plenty of energy for competition. Of course, this also means that the *wrong* foods can slow you down!

The need for nutrients

Food and drink are important because they provide the body with nutrients. There are three main kinds of nutrient: carbohydrates, fats and proteins. Each of these has specific jobs:

- Carbohydrates are a key source of energy for fast movement. They provide glycogen, the energy store held in the muscles and liver. The body's glycogen stores are used during high-speed exercise.

Athletes training for speed-based sports need to eat plenty of carbohydrates, such as potatoes, pasta, rice, low-fat milk, yoghurt, beans and pulses. This helps them to replace the muscle glycogen used during training. At competition time, eating plenty of carbohydrates makes sure the muscles contain as much glycogen as possible.

- Fats are a second source of energy, but not an important one for speed-based sports.

- Proteins help the body to grow, and to repair itself if damaged. They are important for speed-based sports. Proteins are used at a greater rate than normal during high-intensity training, and need to be replaced.

Proteins are especially important for people working on improving their strength, whose muscle fibres will be growing. This has led to a myth that eating extra protein will make your muscles grow – this is not true. It is the training that increases the muscle mass, not the protein!

A good breakfast for a sportsperson, mixes foods that will give a quick burst of energy with foods that have a slower effect.

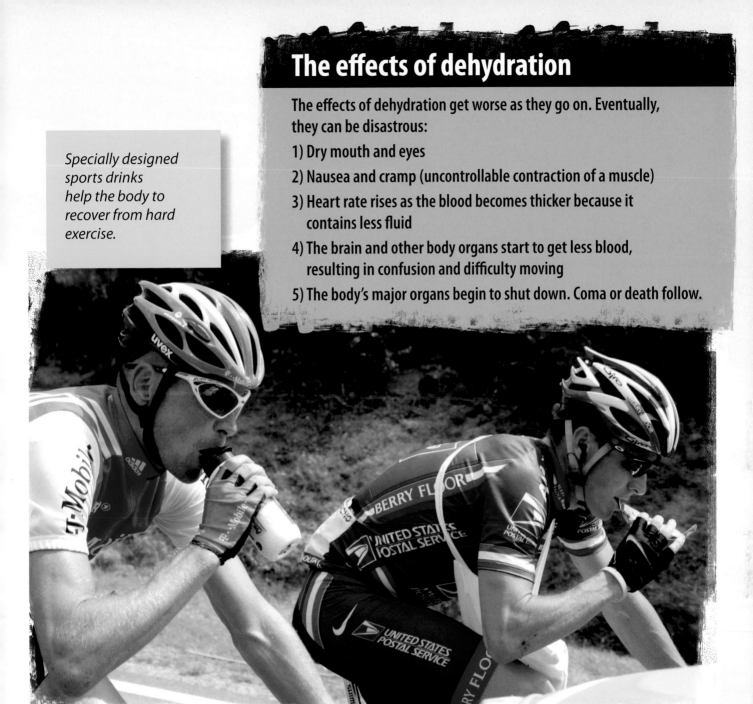

The effects of dehydration

The effects of dehydration get worse as they go on. Eventually, they can be disastrous:

1) Dry mouth and eyes

2) Nausea and cramp (uncontrollable contraction of a muscle)

3) Heart rate rises as the blood becomes thicker because it contains less fluid

4) The brain and other body organs start to get less blood, resulting in confusion and difficulty moving

5) The body's major organs begin to shut down. Coma or death follow.

Specially designed sports drinks help the body to recover from hard exercise.

Hydration

When people exercise, their muscles work harder and generate heat. The body tries to get rid of this heat by sweating. But sweating doesn't only get rid of heat: it also gets rid of important chemicals called electrolytes. These help the muscles contract and relax, so losing them affects performance.

Specialist sports drinks can be more effective than water at replacing the fluids, electrolytes, carbohydrates and proteins that are used during exercise. They usually come in powdered form, which is mixed with water, then shaken. Some athletes make up their own sports drink, using ⅓ fruit juice, ⅔ water and a pinch of salt.

Glossary

ADP
Adenosine diphosphate, a chemical created when the body produces energy.

ATP
Adenosine triphoshate, a chemical that provides living things with energy.

BMX
Bicycle motocross, a bike race over a short course that includes jumps and banked turns.

central nervous system
Brain and spinal cord, which together control and coordinate the body's movements.

coma
long period of unconsciousness, a little like being asleep but unable to wake up.

contract
tighten and pull together.

coordination
skilful and efficient movement of different parts of the body at the same time.

decade
period of ten years' time.

drills
repeated movement designed to improve technique at a sport or physical activity.

efficient
done without wasting any energy.

elastic
able to stretch and return to its original shape.

elite
top-level. In sports, the elite athletes are the best.

flexibility
ability to move joints through a wide range of movement.

hypertrophy
increase in size through growth in size of cells, rather than the number of cells. In muscle hypertrophy, the fibres the muscles are made of get bigger.

joint
part of the body where bones are connected. Many joints can be moved using muscles; others, such as joints in our skulls, cannot.

judoka
person who takes part in judo.

lactic acid
acid in muscles produced during anaerobic exercise, which makes it hard for the muscles to contract efficiently.

lead-out man
cyclist who leads the way to the finish for a team's top sprinter, before peeling off to allow him or her to win.

mobilise
get moving in order to be ready for activity.

nausea
feeling of sickness or that you are likely to vomit.

nutrients
parts of food that allow a human body to work, and help it to grow and repair itself.

organ
body part with a special function. For example, the heart is the organ responsible for pumping blood around the body.

plyometrics
exercises using movements such as jumps to build up strength and power.

professional
paid to do an activity or sports.

proportions
differing levels of parts that make up a whole. For example, sweet drinks have a high proportion of sugar in them.

range of movement
amount of movement possible from one extreme to the other.

resistance
force that slows down another. The fluid inside muscles causes higher resistance to movement until it is warmed up.

rookie
person in their first year of activity. The word is most often used in sports: a player spending his or her first year as a professional or in a new league is known as a rookie.

stages
separate parts of a long race. The word comes from cycling, in which each day's racing is known as a stage.

sustain
continue something for a certain period of time.

velodrome
cycling track, usually an oval shape with banked turns at the end of the straights.

visualization
imagining a good technique or result as a way of helping it to happen.

Further information

BOOKS TO READ

Body: An Amazing Tour of Human Anatomy by Robert Winston (editor) (Dorling Kindersley, 2005)

The Complete Guide To Sports Training by John Shepherd (A&C Black, 2006)
This book has useful workouts for a variety of sports, and a good section on speed training.

The Complete Guide to Strength Training by Anita Bean (A&C Black, 2008)
A former British Bodybuilding Champion gives a wealth of advice about building up muscle strength. The book it strong on weight training, and contains useful weight sessions for a variety of sports.

Goal! Science Projects With Soccer; Wheels! Science Projects With Bicycles, Skateboards and Skates by Madeline Goodstein; and *Slam Dunk! Science Projects With Basketball*, by Robert Gardner and Dennis Shortelle (Enslow Publishers, 2009)

Plyometrics for Explosive Speed and Power by Neal Pire (Ulysses Press, 2006)
Aimed at sportspeople of all abilities and levels, this excellent book contains basic information about plyometrics, plus over 70 exercises. There are specific sets for basketball, cycling, gymnastics, rugby, football, swimming, track and field, and more.

Sports Science by various authors (Franklin Watts, 2009)
A series that takes a look at popular sports, such as football and tennis, and the science behind them.

Sports Science: Why Science Matters by Andrew Solway (Heinemann Library 2009)

Our Bodies by Steve Parker (Wayland, 2006)
This series provides the essential knowledge about anatomy you need as a sportsperson.

WEBSITES TO VISIT

www.brianmac.co.uk/
Brian Mac is a senior coach for UK Athletics, the governing body for track and field in the UK. He has 40 years of experience as an endurance athlete, and over 25 years as a coach, and most of his experience is found somewhere on this exhaustive, but easy to navigate, website.

www.sport-fitness-advisor. com/speedtraining.html
This section of the sport fitness advisor site has basic information on the requirements of speed training, plus links to a huge variety of articles on improving your sprinting technique, drills for speed and agility, speed endurance and much more.

31

Index

TRAINING FOR SPORT

Contents of titles in series:

WAYLAND

Improving
STRENGTH
AND POWER

Paul Mason

WAYLAND

First published in 2010 by Wayland

Wayland
Hachette Children's Books
338 Euston Road
London NW1 3BH

Wayland Australia
Level 17/207 Kent Street
Sydney, NSW 2000

Editor: Julia Adams
Designer: Tim Mayer, Mayer Media
Proofreader and indexer: Claire Shanahan
Picture researcher: Kathy Lockley
Consultant: Professor John Brewer

British Library Cataloguing in Publication Data

Mason, Paul, 1967-
  Training for sport.
  Improving strength.
  1. Muscle strength--Juvenile literature. 2. Physical
  fitness--Nutritional aspects--Juvenile literature.
  I. Title
  613.7'1-dc22

ISBN: 9780750261425

Printed in China

Wayland is a division of Hachette Children's Books,
an Hachette UK company.

www.hachette.co.uk

Websites
The website addresses (URLs) included in this book were valid at the time of going to press. However, because of the nature of the Internet, it is possible that some addresses may have changed, or sites may have changed or closed down since publication. While the author and publisher regret any inconvenience this may cause the readers, no responsibility for any such changes can be accepted by either the author or the publisher.

Disclaimer
During the preparation of this book, all due care has been taken with regard to the advice, activities and techniques described and depicted. The publishers regret that they can accept no liability for any loss or injury sustained.

Picture acknowledgements:
Al Bello/Getty Images: 9
Robert Cianflone/Getty Images: 14
Michael Cole/Corbis: 28TR
Andy Crawford: 15TR
Mark Dadswell/Staff/Getty Images: 29
empipe/Shutterstock: 26 (top)
FRANCK FIFE/AFP/Getty Images: Title page, 8
Chris Floyd/Reportage/Getty Images: 20
foodfolio/Alamy: 28BL
Bill Greenblatt/Liaison/Getty Images: 25
Paul Hanna/Reuters/Corbis: 22-23B
Frederic Haslin/TempSport/Corbis: 23CL
huaxiadragon/iStock: background images throughout
AdrianHillman/iStock images: folios throughout
Alexander Ishchenko/Shutterstock: COVER (small, top)
JeP /Shutterstock: COVER (small, bottom)
Herbert Kratky/Shutterstock: COVER (small, middle)
Robert Kwiatek/Rex Features: 13
Barry Lewis/Corbis: 19
Tom Lynn/Sports Illustrated/Getty Images: COVER, 5
Chris McGrath/Getty Images: 24
Robert Michael/Corbis: 6
MistikaS/iStock: background images throughout
KAZUHIRO NOGI/AFP/Getty Images: 4
ogergo/iStock: background images throughout
ED OUDENAARDEN/AFP/Getty Images: 15
prism68/Shutterstock: 26 (bottom)
Quinn Rooney/Getty Images: 7, 21
EVARISTO SA/AFP/Getty Images: 17
Filip Singer/isifa/Getty Images: 27B
Keren Su/China Span/Getty Images: 22CR
Topham Picturepoint/TopFoto.co.uk: 11
AHMAD YUSNI/AFP/Getty Images: 12

Contents

What is strength?

Strength is the ability to push against resistance. Try and push a car up a hill, and you meet resistance. To overcome it, you need to be very strong indeed. Weightlifters are strong – they can pick up over 400 kilograms. That's the equivalent of two men sitting on each end of the bar (four men in total)!

Strongman competitors, as you might guess, need tremendous maximum strength. They use it for picking up giant stones, pulling trucks and throwing weights high into the air. But where does their strength come from? It comes from their muscles.

China's Linlin Deng competes at the 2008 Beijing Olympics. Gymnasts need to be strong, but in a different way from a weightlifter.

Strength and muscles

Muscles are the parts of your body that move your joints, the places where bones meet. Wrap your left hand around your upper right arm, then lift your right fist towards your shoulder. You will feel the muscle on top of your arm (called your biceps) contracting as it pulls the joint closed. Then, as you lower your arm, your biceps relaxes and your triceps (the muscle on the bottom) contracts.

Your strength is mainly decided by the size and number of the fibres that make up your muscles. It is also linked to the type of fibres the muscles contain. Muscles contain fast-twitch and slow-twitch fibres. Fast-twitch ones are used when more than 25 per cent of your maximum strength is needed. Some people have more fast-twitch fibres than others, and these people are best suited to sports involving speed, strength and power.

Body types

Your body type also affects how much strength you can develop. Some people are born with genes that mean they naturally grow up to be broad and thick-bodied, with large muscles all over their body. But if that isn't you, don't despair! It's possible for everyone to improve their strength, given the right knowledge and training.

Naim Suleymanoglu, on his way to winning a third Olympic weightlifting gold, at the Atlanta Games in 1996.

Naim Suleymanoglu

Sport: Weightlifting

Country: Turkey

Born: 23 January 1967

Proof that you don't have to be big to be strong, Suleymanoglu was known as The Pocket Hercules during his weightlifting career. Suleymanoglu was born in Bulgaria, but from a Turkish family. He first became famous when he set a world weightlifting record when he was just 16 years old.

After being forced by Bulgaria's rulers to change his name to the more Bulgarian-sounding Shalamanov, Suleymanoglu left the country in 1986. He became a Turkish citizen, and Turkey paid Bulgaria US$1,000,000 so that Suleymanoglu could compete for Turkey at the Olympics. He soon repaid the debt:

- In 1988, 1992 and 1996, Suleymanoglu won gold medals in the featherweight weightlifting division.
- He also won the World Championships seven times, the European Championships six times, and set 46 world records.

Suleymanoglu retired in 2000, after failing to win a fourth Olympic gold at the Sydney Games.

Strength in sport

Strength is important in a wide variety of sports. But athletes need to develop different kinds of strength, depending on the sport they take part in. Footballers, strongmen and cricketers all need to be strong in different ways, for example. So, what are the different kinds of strength, and what types of sport are they most useful for?

Maximum strength

Maximum strength is what most people probably think of when they hear the word 'strength'. It describes the maximum amount of force an athlete can generate in one muscle contraction.

Maximum strength is most important in events such as weightlifting and strongman contests. In these, the athletes must pick up or move heavy weights in a single movement. All their muscles together must generate the biggest possible force.

Power

Power is the ability to generate force quickly, with a fast muscle contraction. Power is important in speed-based events, such as:

- Sprinting (on foot, on a bike or in the water)
- Gymnastics, ice skating and other sports that need explosive power as part of their routine.
- Combat sports, such as boxing, judo and taekwondo.

Strength endurance

Strength endurance is the ability to develop force repeatedly. Football midfielders, bowlers in cricket, or tennis players, for example, have to perform the same action again and again. To keep doing so with the same force, they need good strength endurance.

Sprinters need explosive strength to fire themselves out of the starting blocks.

Weight training

One of the most common ways of developing strength is through weight training. It is important that weight training is adapted to the type of strength you want to develop, because each type of strength develops in a slightly different way. Developing tremendous maximum strength is less important for a footballer, for example, than working on power.

Rebecca Romero on track for another Olympic medal, at the Beijing Olympics in 2008.

PROFESSIONAL PROFILE

Rebecca Romero

Sport: Rowing, cycling

Country: UK

Born: 24 January 1980

Romero is a very unusual athlete, having reached the top level at not one but two extremely demanding sports: rowing and cycling. Both sports demand a tricky combination of power and endurance.

Romero's first sport was rowing, in which she won a silver medal at the 2004 Athens Olympics. She retired from rowing with a back injury in 2006.

Like rowing, cycling requires powerful leg and shoulder muscles. Romero found it relatively easy to adapt, and she was good enough to win World Championship gold in both individual and team pursuit.

Romero went to the 2008 Olympic Games as one of the red-hot favourites. She was also the first-ever British woman to compete in two different sports at summer Olympics. When she won gold in the individual pursuit, Romero became only the second woman in history to get medals for two different summer Olympic sports.

Body shapes

All of us are born with slightly different genes. Genes make up the code inside your body that decides things such as the colour of your eyes and hair. Genes also decide what shape your body will be – and this can have a big effect on the kind of sport you are likely to be good at. Scientists divide body shapes into three extremes: endomorph, ectomorph and mesomorph.

Endomorphs

An extreme endomorph has a pear-shaped body, with wide hips and shoulders, and is thicker front-to-back than side-to-side. They carry a lot of body fat on their upper legs, body and upper arms.

Endomorphs are typically able to develop tremendous strength. They are ideally suited to strength sports such as weightlifting, strongman, and hammer and discus throwing. Because of their weight, endomorphs tend to be less good at running sports, but their large lungs may help them to become good at sports such as rowing.

Ectomorphs

Ectomorphs are almost the opposite shape to endomorphs. They have narrow shoulders, chest and hips, long, slim arms and legs, and have very little fat on their body.

Ectomorphs are best suited to endurance sports such as distance running, where their low

Australian hooker Stephen Moore uses his strength to power through a tackle in a 2009 match against France. Rugby has positions for athletes of all shapes and sizes, from endomorphic props and hookers to ectomorphic lock forwards.

weight is an advantage. They find it difficult to build muscle mass, so strength sports present severe challenges to ectomorphs.

Mesomorphs

Mesomorphs have a triangular body, with wide shoulders and narrow hips. They carry little body fat, and are well muscled on their arms, legs and body. Mesomorphs adapt well to training, so they are able to include more strength, power or endurance work, depending on what sport they are taking part in.

Almost there! Matthias Steiner, split seconds away from Olympic glory in 2008.

Matthias Steiner

Sport: Weightlifting

Country: Austria, Germany

Born: 25 August 1982

Matthias Steiner's story is a rollercoaster ride of great achievements and great sadness. He has overcome terrible setbacks to become Olympic champion in weightlifting.

Steiner was born in Austria, and spent his career up until 2005 competing as an Austrian. Despite being diagnosed with diabetes at the age of 18, he was determined to train as a weightlifter.

In 2005, Steiner fell out with the Austrian weightlifting federation. At the same time he met and fell in love with a German woman, Susann. He moved to Germany and apply for German citizenship. This meant it would be three years before he could enter international competitions again.

In 2007, Susann was tragically killed in a car accident. The next year, at the Beijing Olympics, Steiner was determined to put in a performance that would honour his wife's memory. Despite going into the final round of lifts behind, he put in a monumental effort to clean and jerk 258 kg. It was enough to overtake the remaining competitors. As he was awarded his gold medal, Steiner clutched a photo of his wife.

9

Somatotyping

Somatotyping is a way of describing your body type using numbers. It is useful because none of us is a pure endomorph, mesomorph or ectomorph. We all have a bit of each type. Because each body type is better suited to particular sports, knowing your somatotype score can be useful in deciding what kind of sport you are most likely to be good at.

Somatotype scoring

Somatotyping gives you a score according to how strongly you have the characteristics of each body type. With hardly any of the characteristics, you score a 1. With all of the characteristics, you score a 7, the maximum. The scores are given in the order endomorph, mesomorph, ectomorph. A pure endomorph would have a score of 711, a mesomorph would score 171, and an ectomorph 117.

Somatotype diagrams

A somatotype diagram looks a bit like a pyramid, with mesomorphic bodies at the tip. As the body shape trickles down the left or right, the type of sport that the subject is likely to be best at changes. Along the left side are the maximum-strength athletes: wrestlers, strongmen, and weightlifters. On the right are those who would be best at endurance sports.

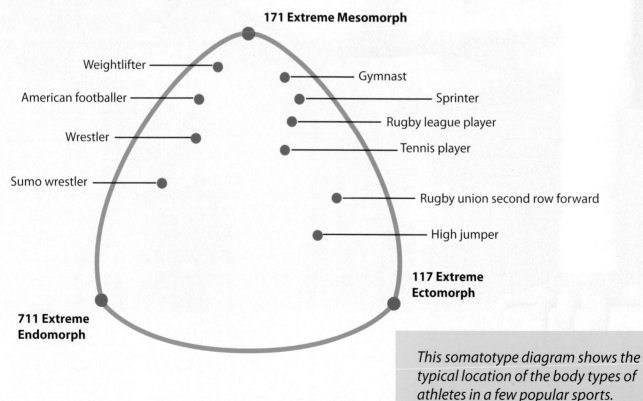

171 Extreme Mesomorph

Weightlifter

Gymnast

American footballer

Sprinter

Rugby league player

Wrestler

Tennis player

Sumo wrestler

Rugby union second row forward

High jumper

117 Extreme Ectomorph

711 Extreme Endomorph

This somatotype diagram shows the typical location of the body types of athletes in a few popular sports.

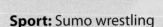

Konishiki

Sport: Sumo wrestling

Country: Hawaii, USA; Japan

Born: 31 December 1963

Konishiki is a Hawaiian-born expert in the Japanese martial art of sumo wrestling. He was the first foreign-born sumo ever to reach the rank of *ozeki*, the second-highest grade. Konishki – whose nickname was The Dump Truck – was also the heaviest sumo ever.

Konishiki originally wanted to become a lawyer, but went to Japan to train as a sumo at the age of 18. He rose quickly to the rank of *ozeki* before knee injuries – made worse as his weight increased to over 250 kg – caused his career to stall.

Konishiki made a brilliant comeback from injury, and by March 1992 he had a recent tournament record of 38 wins and 7 losses. He had also won three major championships. Promotion to *yokozuna*, sumo's highest rank, seemed certain. But in his next tournament, The Dump Truck won only 9 of his 15 bouts, and promotion never came.

Konishiki retired in 1997, and is still a popular celebrity in Japan. He has appeared in several TV shows and movies, and worked as a radio DJ. Konishiki is also a keen musician, mixing rap and ukulele playing in an unlikely combination.

Konishki faces up to a small-but-determined opponent, who doesn't seem to be making much progress.

Strength and weight

All athletes have to balance the need for strength against weight and endurance. Strength comes from big, heavy muscles, which use up energy like a space rocket heading for orbit. Smaller muscles are more like a moped. It may not be as powerful as a space rocket – but it would get you a lot further on the same amount of fuel.

Adapting weight training

Many athletes use weight training to improve the way their muscles work. How they do this must be adapted to the kind of sport they do:

- Pure strength events require big, powerful muscles that can generate high maximum power. These are built up using heavy weights, with each exercise done just a few times.

- If speed-endurance is an important part of your sport, slightly lighter weights are most useful. The exercises will be repeated more times: this helps build up the muscle's ability to keep working for longer.

- For endurance athletes, strength and power are less important than the ability to keep working for a long time. They use lighter weights, with the exercises done a greater number of times.

Mariusz Pudianowski competes in a strongman competition is Kuala Lumpur, Malaysia. This particular event is known as the 'Farmer's Walk'.

Body mass

Muscle fibres are dense and relatively heavy, so increasing the size of your muscles increases your body mass. After a long period of strength training, the scales may read higher – 68 kg instead of 65 kg, for example – even though you are in better shape. This may seem a bit surprising, but it is nothing to worry about unless the increase is large.

The increase in body mass caused by strength training has an important side effect. Many health professionals assess body weight using charts that allow them to look along a line according to a patient's height, and discover whether they are underweight, the correct weight or overweight. Strength athletes often come out as overweight on these charts – even though they are fit and healthy.

Don't try this at home: Pudzianowski takes a 41-tonne airplane for a walk.

Mariusz Pudzianowski

Sport: Strongman
Country: Poland
Born: 7 February 1977

Pudzianowski is one of the world's greatest strongman competitors. He has won the World's Strongest Man title five times – more than anyone else – and goes by the nickname Super Mariusz.

Strongman contests make very specific demands of the competitors. Some come from weightlifting backgrounds, but most specialise in strongman competitions. Events include pulling trucks along on a rope, picking up cars, carrying giant rocks, and throwing heavy weights over high bars.

Pudzianowski won the World's Strongest Man in 2002 and 2003. The second year, he won by the biggest-ever amount. In 2004 Pudzianowski placed third, but was later disqualified for using illegal drugs. Over the years, many people in power-based events have been caught using illegal drugs, particularly anabolic steroids and stimulants, to improve their performance. He was banned from competing for one year.

Pudzianowski returned from his ban as formidable as ever. He won World's Strongest Man again in 2005, 2007 and 2008.

Core stability

Core stability describes the strength of the muscles that support your body's trunk or torso. It is also sometimes called core strength. The most important core muscles are the ones that support the spine. Core stability is important to all sportspeople, because it affects both strength and technique.

Core stability and strength

Core stability is particularly important for people taking part in strength-based sports. For example, imagine a weightlifter doing the clean and jerk. They need powerful arm, shoulder and leg muscles that work together to pick up a heavy weight. But if the lifter's core muscles are weak, then the connection between upper and lower body will buckle under the strain. However strong their arms and legs, the lifter's core will be a weak link in the chain, and will limit their performance.

Core stability and technique

Good core stability is needed in all sports, because it has an effect on how efficiently an athlete can put their technique into action. As an example, imagine a kayaker in a slalom race. They have to paddle strongly for speed, but also to keep the boat as steady and smooth in the water as possible. Without strong muscles in their torso, this would be impossible.

Jenna Myers of Australia showing good weightlifting technique. Her back is straight and her arms fully extended, so that her legs can power the lift.

In many sports – for example, discus throwing, judo or gymnastics – using core muscles as part of your technique adds extra strength and power.

Core stability and injury

Good core stability helps prevent injuries, by making it less likely that the body will be twisted in a dangerous way. In particular, it helps prevent injury to the spine or spinal muscles.

The twists and turns of judo competition demand excellent core strength, whether you are defending or attacking.

Test your core stability

Put a watch on the ground where you can see it. Assume a press-up-like position, forearms flat on the ground and on your toes. It is important to keep your back straight throughout these exercises. Apart from the first and last exercises, try to hold each position for 15 seconds:

- Hold the basic position for 60 seconds
- Now lift your right arm off the ground and hold the position
- Return to the basic position, then lift your left arm off the ground
- From the basic position, next lift your right leg off the ground
- Return to the basic position, then lift your left leg off the ground
- Next lift your left leg and right arm off the ground
- Return to the basic position, then lift your right leg and left arm off the ground
- Go back to the basic press-up position and hold it for 30 seconds

If you can do this, you have good core strength. If not, repeating the routine 3 or 4 times a week will help you to improve. Measure progress in how close to the 15-second timings for each position you can get, or how far through the routine you can get.

Increasing strength

Muscles improve their performance when they are forced to work harder than normal. To improve a muscle's strength, most athletes use weight training, resistance training or a combination of the two.

Resistance training

Resistance training is when the muscle or muscles are trying to overcome an opposing force greater than the one they would usually meet. One of the simplest examples is trying to run through water, which offers more resistance than air. Another is the swim-bench, on which swimmers lie to practise their strokes, by pulling on paddles attached to pulleys. The pulley can be set to feel like the resistance swimmers feel in water, or it can be set to offer greater resistance. Other resistance-training devices include exercise bikes and rowing machines.

Weight training

The most popular way to increase muscle size is through weight training. It is possible to target very specific muscles and groups of muscles using weight training. Athletes rely on their coaches to help them do this, but there is also advice on sources of weight-training workouts for specific sports on page 31 if this book.

Tennis players develop very specific strength in their racquet arm and shoulder, allowing them to add power to their strokes.

Physical effects of strength training

Strength training has three key effects on the body:

1) Muscle hypertrophy – an increase in the size of the individual fibres that make up a muscle

2) An increase in the size and density of bones (which steadily become stronger to bear the extra load)

3) An increase in the amount of energy stored in the muscles, which the body calls on during the first 60–120 seconds of hard activity.

When muscles increase in size, they sometimes become less able to make a wide range of movement. This makes it important to combine flexibility work with strength training.

Stepanka Hilgertova powers through the gates at the World Slalom Championships in 2007.

Stepanka Hilgertova

Sport: Kayak slalom

Country: Czechoslovakia, Czech Republic

Born: 10 April 1968

Stepanka Hilgertova is one of the most successful kayak slalom racers ever. She was at the top of this demanding sport for 16 years, taking part in an amazing five Olympic Games.

Kayak slalom requires great power, as the racers are often forced to turn their boats and paddle upstream, into the teeth of a raging current. They must get the boat going fast enough to carry on through a gate, before swinging round on the current and continuing downstream. To have raced kayak slalom at five Olympics, winning two gold medals, is an amazing achievement.

Hilgertova's Olympic career began in 1992, when she came 12th. At the 1996 Olympics, at the age of 28, she struck gold. This was followed by a second gold in 2000, at the age of 32. Many people would then have retired, but not Hilgertova. She went on to place 5th in the 2004 Athens Games, and 9th in the 2008 Beijing Games. By then, Hilgertova was 40 years old, and eligible to take part in masters competitions!

Training for maximum strength

Maximum strength is usually increased through weight training. Athletes lift close to their maximum possible weight. They perform a small number of repetitions – sometimes as few as one, and rarely more than five – before they have to rest.

Weight training rules

Weight training carries a risk of injury. This is especially true when training to increase maximum strength, because the muscles are working at or near their maximum possible range. It is also possible to damage muscles, tendons and ligaments by doing exercises incorrectly, or simply through an accident in the gym. Following a few basic rules can make weight training much safer:

- Always warm up before weight training. The aim of the warm-up is to increase your body temperature, and to prepare the muscles you are going to be exercising.

- Never train alone: if there's an injury or accident, there won't be anyone there to help.

- Don't over-train (see pages 24 and 25 for more information about this). Allow your body plenty of time to recover from hard training sessions.

1-repetition maximum (1RM)

Weighttraining guides sometimes talk about 1RM, short for 1-reptition maximum. This is the maximum amount of weight an athlete should lift for a particular exercise. It is calculated using a complicated mathematical formula, and is best worked out by a coach.

1RM is a measure of an athlete's strength. If your 1RM figure increases for a particular exercise, it means the muscles used in that exercise are getting stronger.

Repetitions

The number of times you repeat a weight-training exercise is called repetitions. How many repetitions athletes do is governed by what percentage of their 1RM figure they are working at. Training above 80 per cent of 1RM leads to an increase in strength. This table gives a guide to how many repetitions should be done at given percentages:

Per cent of 1RM	Repetitions
60	17
65	14
70	12
75	10
80	8
85	6
90	5
95	3
100	1

Electrical muscle training

Muscle movement is stimulated by a tiny electrical charge from the central nervous system. Research has shown that whichever weight-training activity requires the biggest electrical charge from the central nervous system will produce the biggest gains in muscle growth.

The labels to the diagram show some key muscles, plus the most effective exercise for improving strength in them.

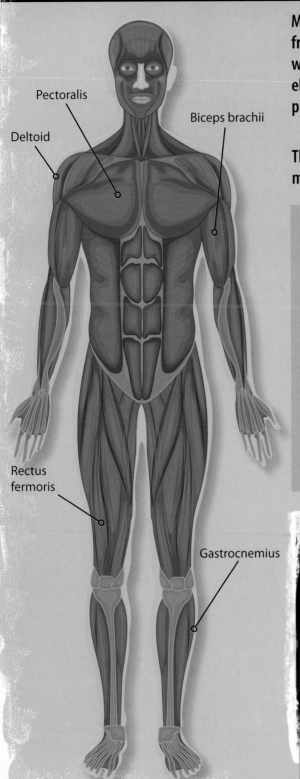

Pectoralis

Deltoid

Biceps brachii

Rectus fermoris

Gastrocnemius

Muscle:	Exercise:
Pectoralis	Dumbbell bench press
Deltoids	Standing dumbbell laterals
Biceps brachii	Incline seated dumbbell curls (alternate)
Triceps	Triceps press down (angled bar)
Latissimus dorsi	One arm dumbbell rows (alternate)
Rectus femoris	Seated leg extensions
Biceps femoris	Standing leg curls
Semitendinosus	Seated leg curls
Gastrocnemius	Standing one leg calf raises

Women generally have less muscle than men, because they have less testosterone, a chemical that helps the body to increase muscle mass. But there are exceptions, such as this competitor at the 1996 British Bodybuilding Championships.

Training for power

In many sports, strength alone is not enough. The strength also needs to be delivered as fast as possible. This kind of strength that allows you to push against something in a fast, strong movement is usually called power. Sprinters, gymnasts, people taking part in combat sports, ice skaters and many other athletes all find that improving their power improves their overall performance.

Targeting fast-twitch muscles

Power training (like all strength training) targets fast-twitch muscle fibres. Most people have roughly 50 per cent fast-twitch and 50 per cent slow-twitch muscle fibres, but some of us have a higher proportion of fast-twitch ones. Those are the people who make it to Olympic finals for the 100 metres, become famous point guards, or make it in the Premier League.

Improving power

Power can be improved in a variety of ways. Weight training improves the athlete's basic strength (see pages 16–19). To add speed, athletes may use some or all of the following:

- plyometrics: the use of jumping, leaping and bounding exercises. These train muscles to produce their strength more quickly.

- complex training: a session of resistance training, followed by plyometric exercises aimed at the same muscles

Former world 100-metres record holder Asafa Powell of Jamaica (in the grey/yellow T-shirt) takes part in plyometric training.

- medicine-ball training: quickly catching and returning a heavy medicine ball, as a way of increasing the speed at which a muscle can work

- conditioning exercises, which help to keep the athlete's entire body working well. These would include core-stability training, and exercises targeted at the athlete's particular sport. A sprinter, for example, might do rat-a-tats: running on the spot on their toes for bursts of 20–30 seconds, lifting their feet just a few centimetres off the ground.

Chris Hoy in full flight, powering round the final bend of a track race.

Chris Hoy

Sport: Track cycling

Country: UK

Born: 23 March 1976

Chris Hoy is, simply, one of the most powerful track cyclists ever. His heavily muscled body and incredible acceleration made him the racer all other riders fear. He is the most successful male Olympic cyclist in history.

As a youngster, Hoy raced BMX (some stories say he was inspired to take it up after seeing the movie *E.T.*). He also rowed for the Scotland junior team. But in 1994 he began concentrating on track cycling. He started to specialise in the 1-km time trial (which is known as the kilo) and the team pursuit.

In 2002, Hoy won team pursuit and kilo gold medals at the world championships. He quickly became the world's best kilo rider. This event demands raw power: Hoy won world titles again in 2004, 2006 and 2007. He also won the Olympic title in 2004.

Hoy's greatest year yet came in 2008. At the Beijing Olympics he won three golds: keirin, team sprint, and individual sprint.

Training for strength endurance

Strength endurance describes an athlete's ability to continue to put out high levels of power over time. For example, imagine two sprinters who can both run 60 metres in seven seconds. But one runs 100 metres in 11.5 seconds, the other runs in 12 seconds. The first runner has better strength endurance. They are able to lay down the power for longer.

Energy for strength

When our muscles have to produce a lot of power quickly, they produce their energy without using oxygen from the bloodstream. This is known as anaerobic energy production. Most people's muscles contain only enough energy stores for between one and two minutes of anaerobic energy production.

A key aim of strength endurance training is to improve the time for which the muscles can work anaerobically. The muscles need to get better at storing and using energy. This happens when the muscles are repeatedly taken into anaerobic energy production.

Lactic acid and fatigue

One by-product of anaerobic energy production is lactic acid. The longer anaerobic exercise goes on, the more lactic acid is produced. Lactic acid causes fatigue – tiredness that makes exercise uncomfortable or painful. In the end, there is so much acid that the muscles cannot work properly.

Improving strength endurance

Weight and resistance training are the most common ways of improving the strength element of strength endurance. One of the most popular ways of improving the endurance element is circuit training.

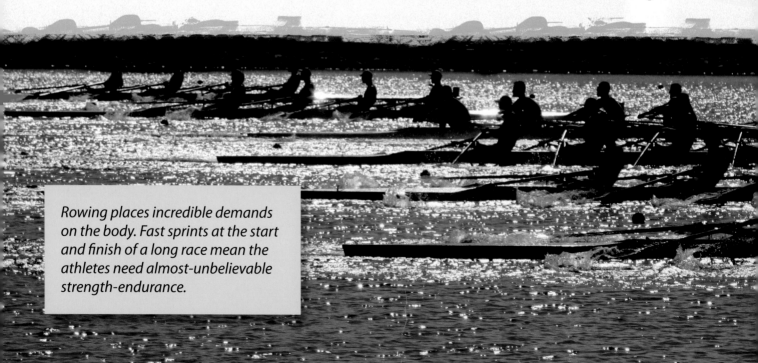

Rowing places incredible demands on the body. Fast sprints at the start and finish of a long race mean the athletes need almost-unbelievable strength-endurance.

In circuit training, between six and 10 strength exercises are done in different zones. The exercises might include press-ups, sit-ups, step-ups and skipping. The athletes do each exercise for a set period of time, then have a brief rest before moving on to the next exercise. Once the circuit of exercises is completed, the athletes have a longer rest before doing another circuit.

A young Steve Redgrave at the 1995 World Rowing Championships, where he won one of his nine World-Championship gold medals.

Steve Redgrave

Sport: Rowing

Country: UK

Born: 10 April 1968

Steve Redgrave is one of the world's most remarkable sportsmen, and the best Olympic rower in history. His biggest achievements are unlikely to ever be equalled:

- Gold medals at 5 consecutive Olympic Games, from 1984 to 2000. Only four athletes have ever managed this feat.
- Nine rowing World Championships gold medals.

Rowers tend to be large and powerful, but even among rowers Redgrave is a big man. He is 1.95 metres tall, and his competition weight was about 100 kg.

Oarsmen usually specialise in rowing either a left or right-side oar. They develop muscles that to allow them to apply maximum power to that specific side of the boat. Redgrave's tremendous natural strength allowed him to row both sides of the boat. He is one of very few rowers to have won Olympic gold medals from both left and right oars.

For most of his career, Redgrave battled against a serious digestive illness. From 1997, he also suffered from diabetes, making his nutrition requirements even more complicated.

Overtraining

In any area of sport, one of the biggest dangers is overtraining. The risks of overtraining are particularly serious in strength training, where muscles and joints are regularly pushed as hard as possible.

Signs of overtraining

Overtraining shows its effects in three key areas, which provide warning signs that an athlete's programme is too demanding:

1) Technique: old technique problems reappear, you find it harder to correct problems, and keeping a rhythm becomes increasingly difficult.

2) Physical condition: tiredness, lack of endurance, physical inability to change or follow tactics during competition.

3) Mental ability: reduced appetite for competition and training, irritability, and inability to accept or act on criticism.

Causes of overtraining

Problems caused by overtraining can result from one or more of the following:

- Not allowing proper recovery times. After a hard training session or competition, your body needs at least 24 hours to recover. Doing more hard training too soon means your body is still tired, so it will be impossible to get near to your highest levels of performance.

- Failing to use light sessions as a vehicle for recovery. All coaches include lighter training sessions in their schedules. These aid recovery, but the athlete must not work harder than planned.

- Making training more demanding too quickly. There are no short cuts in sports training: making training a lot harder each week will just make you more tired, because you are working closer to your maximum.

Kamran Panjayi of Great Britain injures his back at the 2004 Olympic Games in Athens. Injuries can be caused or made worse by overtraining.

It might give you the illusion that you're getting faster, but you won't be.

- Over-competing is a form of overtraining, as it means your body is doing too much work at maximum effort.

- Relying too heavily on a single training method may increase the risk of injury. It makes the muscles that are used more fatigued than a varied training schedule.

- Poor nutrition: not providing your body with the right foods.

- Too much complicated technique work done when tired or without adequate recovery can easily lead to injury.

On your marks... Get set... Magnus ver Magnusson about to start towing a large, heavy truck during a strongman contest.

Magnus ver Magnusson

Sport: Strongman

Country: Iceland

Born: 23 April 1963

Magnus ver Magnusson is a strongman and powerlifter. He won World's Strongest Man contest four times between 1991 and 1996. Magnusson once held the world record for deadlifting a tyre, at 445 kg. That's the same weight as a couple of large mountain gorillas.

Magnusson first took part in a strongman event in 1985, when he finished third in Iceland's Strongest Man. The winner was another great Icelandic strongman (who also won the World's Strongest Man contest four times), Jon Pall Sigmarsson.

Magnusson continued to improve his contest results, and in 1991 he won the World's Strongest title for the first time. Amazingly, it was only after this that he decided to concentrate on strongman contests full-time. He came second in 1992 and 1993, and won the title again in 1994, 1995 and 1996.

Biochememechanics and levers

Biomechanics is the application of mechanical principles to the human body. These principles help us to understand how our bones, joints and muscles work together to provide movement. Knowing this, it is possible for coaches to adjust their athletes' technique so that they get the most from their strength and power.

Biomechanics at work

Some sportspeople at first question how biomechanics can help them to improve their performance. One example of how it helps comes from cycling. Professional cyclists know that the height at which they set their saddle will have a significant effect on their pedalling power:

- If the saddle is too low, the rider will not be able to apply their muscles through a full range of movement. It will also be impossible to use the strong muscles of the cyclist's lower back.

- With the saddle set too high, the cyclist cannot apply full power right through the pedalling action, as their legs will not properly reach the pedals all the time.

- If the saddle is at the right height, power can be applied right through the pedal stroke. The strong muscles of the back and hips can be used as to help power the pedalling movement.

This rider has his saddle too high, as you can see from the way his left foot is forced to stretch down at an angle. As a result, the bottom of his pedal stroke will lack power.

These cyclists have their saddles at an ideal height. They will be able to exert power all the way through their pedal stroke.

The importance of biomechanics to cycling does not end here. For example, above a certain speed, most of a cyclist's energy is used battling air resistance. Adjusting your riding position into a racing crouch makes you more aerodynamic, and therefore faster. But below a certain speed, it is better to sit up straight. This makes it easier to get more air into your lungs, while having only a small cost in terms of air resistance.

Like cycling, all sports involving motion are dependent on good biomechanics for top-level performance.

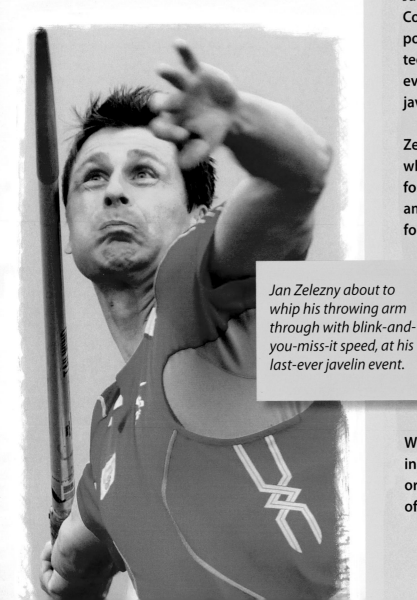

Jan Zelezny about to whip his throwing arm through with blink-and-you-miss-it speed, at his last-ever javelin event.

Jan Zelezny

Sport: Javelin

Country: Czechoslovakia, Czech Republic

Born: 16 June 1966

Jan Zelezny is a hero in his home country of the Czech Republic. There and around the world, he is said by many people to be the greatest javelin thrower ever.

Javelin requires great strength and power. Competitors must have an extremely powerful throwing arm, of course. But their technique also requires them to use almost every muscle in their body in throwing the javelin as far as possible.

Zelezny was famous for the speed with which he could whip his throwing arm forwards, launching the javelin with amazing power. He was also remarkable for his ability to produce his greatest performances at big competitions. He dominated javelin throughout the 1990s, winning Olympics gold at the 1992, 1996 and 2000 Games. Although Zelzny was at his best at the Olympics, he also won three World Championships, in 1993, 1995 and 2001.

World records are broken regularly in athletics, and few last more than a year or two. Remarkably, Zelezny's world record of 98.48 m, set in 1996, still stands.

Nutrition

Good nutrition and hydration are important for everyone's heath, not only athletes'. But sports training places particular demands on the body, which makes it especially important that athletes have a good diet.

A balanced diet

For all of us, a balanced diet is crucial for good health. This means eating the right amounts of specific types of food: carbohydrate, protein and fats. Each of these has a different job to do:

- Carbohydrates are the body's main source of energy. The human body needs about 50–60 per cent of its daily calories to come from carbohydrates.

- Fats are a second source of energy, though a less important one for athletes. No more than 20–25 per cent of your daily calories should come from fats.

- Proteins help the body to grow and to repair itself. We need roughly 15–30 per cent of our daily calories to come from proteins.

Bananas are a great, quick source of energy.

A good meal for an athlete mixes plenty of carbohydrates (pasta, vegetables) with some fat (cheese, for example), and a bit of protein (meat or fish).

The protein myth

Some people think that because proteins help muscles grow, eating more proteins will make their muscles grow bigger. This is incorrect. Muscles grow through working hard: for this they need energy, which they get from carbohydrate. Increasing the percentage of protein you eat will mean your body gets a smaller proportion of carbohydrates, and less energy for training. This won't help your strength increase at all!

Weight gain and loss

When training to increase strength, most people will gain weight. Their muscles, and over the medium to long-term their bones, will grow bigger and more dense.

Strength training is generally not a good way to lose weight. If weight loss is required, however, reducing daily calorie intake by no more than 15 per cent will achieve this. A 15 per cent decrease allows athletes to retain hard-earned muscle, but will make it difficult to increase strength or power.

Halil Mutlu on his way to his third Olympic gold medal in a row, this one at the 2004 Athens Games.

Halil Mutlu

Sport: Weightlifting

Country: Bulgaria, Turkey

Born: 14 July 1973

Halil Mutlu is a Bulgarian-born Turkish weightlifter. He is one of only four weightlifters who have won gold medals at three consecutive Olympic Games.

As a young man of 16, Mutlu moved to Turkey from Bulgaria. He was so pleased to arrive that he changed his name from Huben Hubenov to Halil Mutlu. (Mutlu means 'happy' in Turkish.) In 1994, Mutlu won his first international titles, the European and World Championships. It was the start of a long period at the top of the weightlifting world. His successes included:

- **winning nine European Championships**
- **five World Championship victories**
- **three Olympic gold medals (won in 1996, 2000 and 2004)**
- **more than 20 world records, set in three different weight divisions**

In 2005, Mutlu was banned from competition for two years after testing positive for an illegal anabolic steroid, nandrolone. He claimed never to have knowingly taken drugs, but weightlifting's terrible reputation for drug abuse made people question if this could be true.

Glossary

aerodynamic
able to pass easily through air, without meeting significant air resistance.

air resistance
the slowing-down effect of air as an object passes through it.

anabolic steroids
drugs that can be used to increase muscle mass and strength. The use of steroids in sport is not allowed, because it is risky for athletes' health and gives those who take the drugs an unfair advantage.

anaerobic
without oxygen. Anaerobic energy production happens without the need for oxygen. It produces energy very quickly, but also uses a lot of the muscle's energy stores very quickly.

calorie
measure of the amount of energy contained in food.

central nervous system
brain and spinal cord, which together control and coordinate the body's movements.

clean and jerk
weightlifting technique that allows more weight to be picked up than any other. The lift is done in two stages. First, the lifter pulls the weight up to rest on his or her chest. Second, they thrust it up above their head.

contraction
getting smaller or tightening up.

deadlifting
weightlifting event, in which a heavy object is lifted from the ground to hip height and lowered again in a controlled way.

diabetes
disease of having too much sugar in your blood. This happens because the body stops taking sugar out of blood and turning it into energy stores.

flexibility
ability to move joints through a wide range of movement.

force
physical influence that makes an object move.

genes
code inside your body that decides things such as the colour of your eyes and hair.

joint
part of the body where bones are connected. Many joints can be moved using muscles; others, such as joints in our skulls, cannot.

keirin
track cycling event that began in Japan, but is now raced around the world. The riders at first cycle behind a tiny moped, which slowly begins to travel faster. Shortly before the end of the race, the moped reaches about 50kph and pulls off the track, after which the riders sprint for the finish.

ligament
tough fibres that support a joint and help it to keep its shape.

masters
sports event for older people.

powerlifting
weightlifting event that combines three different kinds of lift, the squat, bench press, and dead lift.

pursuit
cycling race in which two riders start on opposite sides of the track and try to catch one another up. If both fail to do so, the first one to finish a set distance is the winner.

range of movement
amount of movement possible from one extreme to the other.

scull
race with each rower in a boat using two oars, one on each side.

stall
slow down or stop moving forwards.

stimulants
drug that increase the body's activity, mainly by increasing heart rate.

tendon
strong fibre that attaches muscle to bone.

torso
trunk; central part of body, ending at the neck, shoulders and hips.

trunk
see torso.

Further information

BOOKS TO READ

Body: An Amazing Tour of Human Anatomy by Robert Winston (editor) (Dorling Kindersley, 2005)

The Complete Guide To Sports Training by John Shepherd (A&C Black, 2006)
This book has useful workouts for a variety of sports, and a good section on speed training.

The Complete Guide to Strength Training by Anita Bean (A&C Black, 2008)
A former British Bodybuilding Champion gives a wealth of advice about building up muscle strength. The book it strong on weight training, and contains useful weight sessions for a variety of sports.

Goal! Science Projects With Soccer; Wheels! Science Projects With Bicycles, Skateboards and Skates by Madeline Goodstein; and *Slam Dunk! Science Projects With Basketball*, by Robert Gardner and Dennis Shortelle (Enslow Publishers, 2009)

Our Bodies by Steve Parker (Wayland, 2006)
This series provides the essential knowledge about anatomy you need as a sportsperson.

Plyometrics for Explosive Speed and Power by Neal Pire (Ulysses Press, 2006)
Aimed at sportspeople of all abilities and levels, this excellent book contains basic information about plyometrics, plus over 70 exercises. There are specific sets for basketball, cycling, gymnastics, rugby, football, swimming, track and field, and more.

Sports Science by various authors (Franklin Watts, 2009)
A series that takes a look at popular sports, such as football and tennis, and the science behind them.

WEBSITES

www.brianmac.co.uk/
Brian Mac is a senior coach for UK Athletics, the governing body for track and field in the UK. He has 40 years of experience as an endurance athlete, and over 25 years as a coach, and most of his experience is found somewhere on this exhaustive, but easy to navigate, website.

http://www.sport-fitness-advisor.com/speedtraining.html
This section of the sport fitness advisor site has basic information on the requirements of speed training, plus links to a huge variety of articles on improving your sprinting technique, drills for speed and agility, speed endurance and much more.

Index

TRAINING FOR SPORT

Contents of titles in series:

WAYLAND